Surviving the Unthinkable

Surviving the Unthinkable

Choosing to Live After Someone You Love Chooses to Die

Don J. Payne

Foreword by
Gordon MacDonald

RESOURCE *Publications* · Eugene, Oregon

SURVIVING THE UNTHINKABLE
Choosing to Live After Someone You Love Chooses to Die

Resource Publications
An Imprint of Wipf and Stock Publishers
199 W. 8th Ave., Suite 3
Eugene, OR 97401

www.wipfandstock.com

ISBN 13: 978-1-4982-3063-6

Manufactured in the U.S.A.   09/28/2015

To my family

Table of Contents

Foreword

SOME MONTHS AGO, OUR oldest granddaughter, Erin, a college senior, called to say that a personal friend of hers had ended his life. To describe her as distraught, momentarily inconsolable, would be an understatement. My wife, Gail, and I tried hard to be a source of strength to our granddaughter, but we both shared the troubling feeling that there were many things we simply did not understand as to why one would want to terminate life and what might be the effect upon those who are known as *suicide-survivors.*

Then, just a few days after Erin's phone call, a good friend, Dr. Don Payne, reached me and asked if I would consider writing a brief foreword to a book which was to be titled, *Surviving the Unthinkable.* He'd written the book, he said, out of the experience of losing his brother, Bob, to a death by suicide.

Of course, I said yes.

Soon a draft of Don's manuscript was in my hands. I read it straight through—unable to put it down—and was deeply touched. My first thought upon finishing *Surviving the Unthinkable* was that it was exactly what our granddaughter needed while in the grasp of her own deep grief. With Don's permission I immediately emailed my copy to her. A day later Erin phoned me. Her gratitude for the book was immense. As had been my experience, the book had touched her broken heart.

I am confident that that same experience will happen to many others when this wonderful Don-Payne writing reaches them. In one of the book's earliest paragraphs, the author says of himself and his family, "We are now members of a club that no one wants to join." Don goes on to describe exactly what that "club membership" (so to speak) entails. As a storyteller he narrates the horrific chain of events that loved ones, the survivors, experience as they try to make sense of the loss of one whom they have loved and would do anything to have back.

But *Surviving the Unthinkable* is not just a story about emotional and spiritual pain. You see, Don Payne is an experienced theologian, and, calling upon his theological disciplines and extensive knowledge of the Scriptures, he offers a treasure of insights for any reader seeking a way to think about such unspeakable tragedies.

I'm grateful that throughout this book Dr. Payne never attempts to go for easy answers to the matter of suicide. He writes with a startling candor. You can easily detect his paralyzing bewilderment, his unbearable anguish when the call comes informing him that his brother is gone. But there is also an obvious maturity and wisdom that quickly rises to stabilize his tumbling soul.

In the course of the book Don Payne speaks of the evil embedded in the act of suicide. He talks about how it radiates deep hurt into a multitude of people. He puts words like forgiveness, reconciliation, and redemption on the table and offers clarity about how they work. Oh, let me also add: there's a lot of hope in this book. But it's a hope scarred by a torment none of us would ever volunteer to undergo.

I am encouraged by Don Payne's description of the goodness of people (friends) who genuinely cared for him and his grieving family. And I was warmed by what Don calls "weird" (his word-choice) incidents which he doesn't bother to defend but which provoke consoling effects. The reader wonders, *were these weird things also part of God's way of speaking into Don Payne's life?* And the answer as far as I'm concerned? Probably.

Toward the end of this intimate book are interesting bits of counsel that may surprise a reader or two. Samples? Don says "partying" (with good friends, of course) is helpful. Wholesome laughter is important. And for Don Payne anyway, drinking lots of upscale flavored coffee is a must. I would not have expected this last one, but it worked for him.

Let me be frank. Whether or not you are a survivor of a suicidal event, you need to read every word of this book. Don't skim it. Rather, let it trickle down into your soul. That's what I did. And that's what our granddaughter, Erin, did. And, in both of our experiences God spoke powerfully through the words of a special friend.

Gordon MacDonald

Chancellor, Denver Seminary

Preface

IN THE SMALL BOOKCASE directly across from my desk is a book entitled *If You Want to Write*. I have never read it. It belonged, somewhat ironically, to my brother, who envisioned himself as something of a writer—and whose suicide was the occasion for this book. I did not want to write this book. In the course of our lives most of us occasionally stumble across and are forced to face daunting tasks that exhaust our known resources and capacities. I'm not thinking about complex logic problems or tasks of a technical nature like repairing a computer, most of which can be kept at a distance from the core of who we are. Rather, I have in view the more personally overwhelming experiences that jar us at our core in incalculable, unpredictable, disorienting, and sometimes terrifying ways. That is the reason I wrote this book. Whether or not another person would ever read it, I had to write it—for myself if for nobody else.

This modest manuscript has taken me longer to write per word than anything else I have ever written. All in all it has been almost four years (working at it on and off) since I began. That's a long time for such a small book because only periodically could I find the motivation and emotional stamina to work on it. The problem was that writing the book forced me to think about the subject of the book. Admittedly, this is an odd and melancholy way to start a book I would want people to read. However, admitting these struggles provides a platform for gratitude to those who have sustained and loved me through not only the process of writing but also the experience about which I have written.

Most prominent in that fine company of people is my wife Sharon, whose quiet and tender presence was consistently sacramental during my bouts of grief, and who offered helpful insights on the manuscript. Dani, Jim and his wife Hilary, and Robb, four incredible people I'm privileged to have as children—and as friends—prayed for me and loved me as only they could do. Wes Roberts, a wise mentor, provided initial encouragement and wise input for moving ahead with this project when I was unsure whether it should be done at all. Rick Rupp, my friend for thirty-four years has stood with me emotionally more than I could have imagined or asked. Longtime companions Jim Bahl, Kathy and Steve Loomis, Julie and Tom Melton, Bill Morgan, and Carrie Wampler have simply been deeply and powerfully present. Laura Flanders, a highly valued friend and colleague who has walked the same journey I write about, provided much-needed affirmation after reading an early draft of the manuscript. Gordon MacDonald, who graciously agreed to provide the foreword, has embodied grace and wisdom in his care for me. The Denver Seminary community as a whole has been an encouraging and supportive context for this journey. Within that community I owe thanks to many who will not know they did anything at all. None of these remarkable people are to be blamed for any deficiencies in what I write, but they deserve my deepest gratitude for their imprints on my life. Should you find benefit from anything you read here, they have a share in it.

It would be both narcissistic and untrue to present this account primarily as "my" story, even though I'll only dare to speak for myself. Our family and many friends were and are as deeply impacted as I was by my brother's suicide. Each of us lost someone a bit different when we lost him: a brother, a son, a husband, a father, a cousin, a friend, a coworker. I want to honor each person in that circle and recognize the depths of their loss, not merely my own.

With that rather heavy entrance, I must insist that this book aims at hope and gratitude. The other side—the hopeful side—of such an experience does not arrive suddenly in a single package but stretches out along a long path. The words "hope" and "gratitude" may sound more cheery than they actually feel on most days. It should not surprise us that hope and gratitude have multiple facets and that some of those facets are roughly textured. Nor are they singular emotions. Part of that "rough texture" comes from being mixed with constant awareness of our loss—sometimes keen and sometimes dull, but always there as active ingredients alongside hope and gratitude. Moreover, hope and gratitude do not simply arrive and stay with us. They may come and go. With those caveats, let me assure you that they are real and possible. Without that prospect, I would never have written. Along the way, I'll try to explain what they look like.

If you or someone you know has faced the unthinkable—losing to suicide someone deeply loved—mere survival often seems to take every available resource and then some. My goal, my hope, and my prayer for you goes beyond mere survival. I want you to live on the other side. The life I envision for all of us on the other side is a life in which our unthinkable loss, and perhaps unthinkable losses of other types, find a place to exist without dominating us; a life with expanded capacities for faith, hope, and love; a life of durability; a life that is rebuilt over ruins. I pray that God makes that so for you. For that I will be quite grateful.

Introduction

My family and I are suicide survivors. We are those left behind after a deeply loved family member chose to end his own life. In those two sentences I just wrote some of the most difficult words I have ever put together. And perhaps in those two brief statements I have said more per word than with any other collection of words I have written or uttered. The journey of interpreting and surviving our loved one's suicide will never end, I suspect. The experience is too thick, too dense. There is simply too much.

Comparing life to a roller coaster may be cliché, but the analogy fits in numerous ways. The heights provide thrilling, if temporary views. Dramatic plunges induce terror. Intense side-to-side twists leave us with sore muscles. Of course, we ride roller coasters more or less willingly, reasonably confident that the experience is safe. We know that the ride will only last a short time, ending at a secure platform where we can walk away and get ice cream.

The ride through the aftermath of suicide also includes those dramatic emotions and aftereffects but without the comforting knowledge that it will end soon. And there is no fun. Roller coaster enthusiasts can join clubs that promote and celebrate the fun of the coaster experience. We are now members of a club that nobody wants to join. In comparison to the overall human population this is a tiny fellowship. Yet, because of its entrance requirements, it is still far too large. In fact, it should never exist at all. Those who take their own lives leave behind them incalculable ripples of pain and devastation. Perhaps those aftereffects were blurred to our loved ones while they were contemplating their own demise, but those effects are vivid for those who are pummeled by the shock waves of the loss.

As relatively recent inductees to this society, my family and I still have much to learn from members with more seniority. Sadly, we know that others are yet to follow us. They will follow unwillingly, but nevertheless they will join us. We pretend no expertise in navigating this tangled path. A wise friend of mine commented to me less than three weeks before our tragedy that as we face various challenges throughout our lives, we're often doing something for the very first time. For this reason, we can expect the experience to be awkward, unsophisticated, and riddled with questions, confusion, and missteps.

Go to a well-stocked Christian bookstore or look online and you can find plenty of books written to help those left behind a suicide. I scanned a couple of those volumes after our own loss and found each to be wise and helpful in its own way. My intent is not to correct or trump what has already been written. Others who dare to write of such an experience deserve respect and appreciation.

I have one basic goal—to offer a bit of strength and encouragement to others who are forced to deal with a suicide. This goal has three parts: first, I want to give voice to some of the strange and unpredictable emotions that come packaged in such an experience. Second, I will offer some reflections on the experience from the vantage point of Christian faith. Third, I will attempt to point out where hope can be found. That third aspect includes suggestions for meaningfully coming alongside both those who are stumbling through the experience of losing someone to suicide and those who may be somewhere on the path toward taking their own lives, even if they don't know it or give no signs of it.

I offer no grandiose claim that "this is not just another book" on the subject. It is, in fact, just another book on the subject. For all of human history people have experienced bereavement and, I suppose, this particular kind of bereavement. Everything my family and I have experienced, felt, and thought, has been encountered by countless others.

But that's the point. That's how we as human beings come to understand and grow from our painful experiences. We talk about them. We help each other find ways of talking about them. The dignity of our humanity is reflected in that act of talking about things. It's one way we interpret and rise above our losses. We may never "find meaning" in the experiences themselves, especially when they are tragic and irrational, but we can find meaningful ways of being present in those experiences and being present to others who share them.

In regard to the second part of my goal—that is, offering perspective from the vantage point of Christian faith—I must "put my cards on the table." I engage this crushing loss not only as a Christian but also as a seminary professor; I teach theology. Those of us with such a calling routinely attempt to offer interpretations of life from God's perspective. Certainly, the inherent risk in that type of vocation is the temptation to pontificate about matters beyond our personal experience. I hope that my admitting that will not confirm the illusion that theologians live in an "ivory tower," insulated from the "real world." Theologians of all sorts have to pay bills, struggle with kids and illness, mow their lawns, and struggle with relationships and losses just like anybody else.

When I teach theology, I work hard to anchor my theology in the recognizable struggles, joys, and questions of life. In this particular case, however, my theology has been tested in unprecedented ways. I cannot help but process the multiple questions and forms of pain in theological categories. Above all, I need to know where this experience finds a place in God. I confess up front, though, that I don't intend to offer tidy theological resolution to the tangled questions and emotions that befall us when a loved one takes his or her own life.

All the same, I will attempt to offer some theologically shaped musings about my experience. These are meant to give hope without giving answers. Sometimes God gives us answers and sometimes (perhaps often?) he does not. In my own observations, however, trying too hard either to give or to get answers often makes our pain even worse. I think this is because ultimately God himself, in Christ, IS our answer, whether or not we are able to articulate that with satisfying precision. So, our gracious and merciful God may use anything I say in any way he chooses. I will be satisfied with whatever that turns out to be.

In 1977 Sheldon Vanauken published *A Severe Mercy*, the captivating and gut-wrenching autobiographical account of how he and his wife, Davey, came to faith in Jesus Christ—then his subsequent loss of Davey to cancer. When I read his book in 1984, I wept bitterly even though I had nothing in my own life as a touchstone for understanding his pain. Now, even though the circumstances of my loss are different from Vanauken's, I understand a bit more of what the title means. God is merciful, but in ways that defy our expectations, our demands, and even our criteria. That may sound like nonsense to some and there is only so much that anyone like me can do to explain the claim or make it plausible. Yet, I stand by it.

Perhaps it will make more sense as I invite you with me on a sacred path through the most difficult and painful experience of my life thus far. If you have endured (or are enduring) something like it, I pray that my thoughts will be healing even if they cause you to reenter your own loss in some painful manner. If you are close to someone who has walked this path, I hope that you will gain some appreciation, even if from a distance, of the utterly strange world that person now inhabits.

The severity of God's mercy makes it no less merciful. It means, at the very least, that God offers his mercy even in the midst of the most severe circumstances, sustaining what is most central to our lives—faith, hope, and love—without always eliminating the circumstances or consequences that threaten to eclipse those gifts. It also means that mercy and severity seem strangely indistinguishable at times.

Every loss of the type my family and I have known—to a suicide—has unique features as well as common ground with other losses. My family's loss has no privileged status as being more tragic or more intense than anyone else's loss. Any loss of a person is tragic and intense. These losses cannot be quantified and should not be compared. They are unfathomable and incalculable. I hope you will engage my reflections as simply one traveler's log, left behind for the possible encouragement of others. Whatever encouragement and hope it may provide will probably be of a sober sort. Call that a "thick" encouragement, with little that will make you laugh or smile, but might still give you hope and some reason to believe that such losses are not the final word.

The pain and questions thrash us. Some of them never go away. While they inevitably mark us—and deeply so—they need not define us.

Writing a book like this should not suggest that my own journey of grief and questioning has drawn to a close. Far from it. Writing this book has caused me to reenter experiences that, frankly, I would rather put behind me. So, when I invite you to accompany me on a journey, it's not an exciting or invigorating journey for either you or me. In fact, it's awful. But it's a significant and meaningful journey.

Prior to that time when God resolves and restores all things (which I am now more eager for than ever!) . . .

Meaningful does *not* necessarily mean getting answers.

Meaningful does *not* mean things are "OK" or that they are not as bad as we thought.

Meaningful does *not* mean we see some greater purpose in our loss.

Rather, *meaningful* involves being sustained by a measure of confidence (some days more, some days less) that our losses are themselves defined by something greater. We have a place to put them. As Paul indicated in 1 Corinthians 15, death is not the final word. So, even with all those qualifiers, *meaningful* ain't too bad!

As I began writing, it had only been six months since my younger brother took his own life. By psychological and therapeutic "industry standards" that's not very long; certainly not long enough for a grief cycle to have run a full and healthy course. I consulted with a trusted mentor about whether it was too soon for me to begin writing about this. His counsel, which I have chosen to follow, was to let each reflection stand on its own without attempting an overarching argument. The writing has now stretched past the four year mark, where the pain is not gone, but is a bit different. As the book unfolds you may sense something of my own movement over time. I hope that, too, will be of help.

So, if you are further along this particular path of grief than I am as I write any part of this, you may have a different view of what I describe. Remember, though, that my goal is to give voice, not answers. I want to tell my story and offer my reflections as I experienced them along the way. Some aspects may look and feel different to me as time unfolds. However, it has become apparent to me that others on this journey need validation from within the slices of their experience, not only from further down the road.

I will not utilize diagnostic frameworks such as stages of grief. As some have suggested, these stages are not necessarily linear. We don't merely exit one stage and enter the next. Rather, the multiple, complex experiences of grief often overlap and are repeatedly reentered in different ways. Some of my musings may reflect different stages of my own grief experience, though for my purposes it doesn't matter much to me what those stages were at the time. I'm sure that these experiences and reflections connect in some way, but I'll leave those connections and diagnoses to others who are more qualified (and interested) in such matters.

Even for "insiders," my experience may sound a bit different. It may not even be the same as it is for others in my family since my personal sense of loss is certainly conditioned by many factors, including how others cared for me in the aftermath. Yet, despite the variety of factors that shape our experiences of loss, we share a common humanity, a humanity that was not made for this. The loss of a loved one to suicide disrupts us and jars us at our very core. If I could say that any more vividly and forcefully I would. Dressing the wounds and honoring the scars is delicate work. It's holy work if those wounds and scars are to become for us like Jacob's permanent limp became for him after wrestling with the Lord (Genesis 32)—a memorial of having met the Lord. That vision pulls me forward. It's a vision for the completion of what is now experienced only partially and by faith. The word "until" summarizes the consolation that comes from anticipation and promise. If you, too, or someone you know, has been forced to live in the space of *until* . . . I hope you will join me.

1

Restaurants

It had been a good day.

9:30 a.m.	Taught a theology class.
11:00 a.m.	Met with a colleague.
1:00 p.m.	Committee meeting (fairly productive, as committee meetings go).
3:00 p.m.	Taught another class.
5:30 p.m.	My wife, Sharon, swung by to pick me up for an evening out with friends . . .

I remember details of that day; details that normally would have long since faded from memory into that ocean of daily "stuff" that makes up so much of our lives. This day's details would soon stick to an unexpected adhesive inside my mind.

The evening out had been on our calendar for a few weeks and I was eager to kick off the weekend with people I enjoy. We drove about ten miles to a restaurant where most of the group had already gathered. I remember the drive as Sharon and I caught up a bit, sharing what the day had contained for each of us.

Among those vivid though ordinary images in my memory bank is pulling into the restaurant parking lot. I remember taking the right turn . . . letting Sharon off at the door . . . seeing a parking spot (I can still see that space in my mind) . . . pulling in . . . pocketing my keys . . . walking past a few people seated on the outdoor patio . . . entering the restaurant and spotting our party seated to the left. I greeted Danny and Joan; waved at Elodie on the other side of the big table; ordered a drink from the server; grabbed Dave by his shoulder to make a smart remark about his attire . . . then felt my cell phone vibrate in my pocket.

My sister's name was on the caller ID. With the clamor of voices and dishes all around me, I had to step outside a nearby side door in order to take the call. Her distraught voice on the other end immediately signaled trouble. Through her tears she told me that our brother in Florida had just taken his own life.

Quickly I grabbed Sharon, mentioned something brief about the call to her and a couple of others, asking them to pray, and we bolted out of the restaurant. Our senses had not even begun to absorb what we had just been told. We drove back across town in stunned silence to meet my parents and sister. That drive, and almost every turn in it, is still carved in my mind.

From that point on, the evening was much as you might expect under such circumstances. Anguished hugs, tears, bewilderment, shock. Phone calls to inform other family members, contact from church leaders, more phone calls across the country trying to get more information from my brother's wife. It fell to me to make several of these calls. With each one I could barely speak. Our children (all adults) were remarkable. They cried with me. One prayed for me over the phone. I'll treasure those moments for the rest of my life, though it was the darkest, densest, longest evening of my life thus far.

As you might expect, the "why's?" and "if only's" kept assaulting us. We reassured each other as best we could. The evening ended with a gathered prayer. What do you pray at a time like that? "Lord, we hurt and we don't understand any of this. Help us. We trust you with this because that's all we know to do." It went something like that.

The drive home was numb. The force and reality of all this had not yet settled. The most intense grief was still ahead, as we were too stunned and reeling. Perhaps that is part of God's mercy. Our senses can only take so much at a time. Shock seems to have a preservative effect.

The next few days were jammed with flight arrangements, funeral plans, emails, text messages, Facebook posts, and countless other conversations. It was a surreal time, punctuated by these and a laundry list of other tasks—some routine and some created by the tragedy. Even while living a nightmare, the bed still had to be made. The dishwasher still had to be loaded. The dog still had to be fed. Strange!

In all of this we simply tried to be with each other as a family every day. In some sense it was hard to be together but we needed it. I wondered whether from this point forward it would always be painful to be together as a family. Would we always remind each other of our loss, at least silently? I suspected so. This will now likely be a distinct thread in the fabric of our relationships, an unspoken subtext to our times together, however much we might laugh and have fun.

Even if this loss was not to define us, I knew it would mark us indelibly. Even if the loss was to be redeemed, it would not be reversed. It has happened and nothing will make it "unhappen." Daily activities and plans are now seasoned forever by that one phone call. As our lives go forward we will continue to do many of the same things we have always done. Yet, one action, one choice by one of us has now somehow touched every ordinary experience, every task, and altered the future script of each one who remains.

After a long flight we gathered with my sister-in-law's family on the other side of the country. We cried. We ate. We laughed (a strange and even holy phenomenon at such a time; still not sure I comprehend it). We talked about my brother and his choice, sometimes directly, sometimes indirectly (indirection allows you to deal with pain and still survive). We prepared for the funeral as best we could. We braced ourselves.

The family visitation at the funeral home utterly unraveled us for a short time; at least it did me. I've never felt such an intense and simultaneous mixture of grief and rage as I walked into the funeral parlor and saw the closed casket that held my brother's body. The beautiful, enlarged photograph of him and his lovely wife stood nearby on an easel. The video collage tastefully prepared by the funeral home, complete with patriotic musical background (he was a veteran), was more than I could bear. I wept with gut-wrenching force. After gaining a measure of composure, we received visitors.

Genuine concern expressed by people I had never met afforded an odd sort of comfort. I did not know them but they knew my brother, so we were strangely connected. Due to the different contexts and time frames, they knew a different person than I knew. Yet, we knew the same person. They worked with him. They watched him in action. They respected him.

But *I* grew up with him. When we were kids, *I* picked on him and "tattled" on him. *I* hugged him and wrestled with him. *I* fought with him as only brothers can do. *I* drove around with him in a rental car only a year and half earlier after our grandmother's funeral, reminiscing about our childhood memories. *I* laughed with him as only brothers can laugh together. *I* loved him.

The next day I had the horrible honor of officiating at his funeral service. I remember waking that morning and the feel of my feet touching the floor as I got out of bed. At that moment I thought to myself, "I'm about to conduct my own brother's funeral service." Talk about bizarre! Among the strange experiences that marked that day were sitting in his study, at his desk, with his mail piled on my left side, finalizing my remarks for his funeral.

In several years of pastoral ministry I've officiated at quite a few funerals and memorial services. Those are sacred occasions and I've always attempted to be genuinely sympathetic with the bereaved. That turns into a complex challenge when you are both the minister and one of the bereaved; when you realize that you have to put on your "game face" and lead your own family through such a wrenching occasion.

Some of my grieving had to be put on hold. Knowing that I would be able to grieve until the night before the service and then again afterward, I leaned into the gritty task of being with my family while being detached just enough that I could do what I needed to do with some measure of composure. I have never prayed more fervently for God to undergird me.

There is nothing quite like walking your own family down the aisle of a funeral home chapel, seating them, taking the podium to face them, and then talking to them about someone you knew and loved as much as they did. One of my best friends marched with our family and sat with my parents, his arm around my dad when I could not be by him to do what a son is supposed to do.

What do you say and what are you supposed to feel when the one you loved, the one you mourn, is both victim and perpetrator? How do you enter that moment as one who also needs to grieve, who also needs to hear the Word of God, who also needs to receive, who also needs the freedom to be broken? How do you restrain your emotions enough to get through the occasion, yet without being stoic? How do you speak the Word of God when your own world has been flipped upside down? How is a person supposed to do that?

Struggling through this somehow (certainly by God's grace), I then had to repeat it in condensed form across the street at a graveside service. Ironically, there are no words to describe the experience of speaking the very last words that would be publicly spoken over your loved one's body; watching the dignified yet painfully slow process of a naval officer folding a flag and presenting it to a widow; listening in silence to the piercing mournfulness of "Taps."

What began at a restaurant ended (at least that day's episode ended) at another restaurant. God's mercies can feel as strange as they are severe and as strange as the tragedies that befall us. After the conventional reception in the family home, we excused ourselves and drove to the ocean with our close friends. We removed our shoes and walked the beach, then found a seafood restaurant sitting on a pier over the water.

With the sun fully set, the restaurant windows open, the ocean breeze softly moving over us, and a brilliant full moon reflecting brightly off the ocean surface, we knew God's merciful presence in that moment. It was more than a sensation; it was a sacrament—a gift from God that touched the recesses of our fractured and hemorrhaging hearts.

For a few hours that evening we knew peace. It was not a peace that continued uninterrupted or that insulated us against the painful grieving process yet to come. Instead, it was like a piton one might come across in a steep rock face, hammered in there by someone else and appearing at just that instant when you desperately needed something to grab.

Stable handholds like that can save our lives—even repeatedly—but we can't live day in and day out clinging only to pitons. We must eventually figure out how to get off the steep, treacherous rock face and onto more reliable footing. Yet, the climb to more level ground may still be long and exhausting, bringing more falls, scrapes, and bruises. Over eastbound I-70, coming out of the Rockies and approaching Denver, hangs a sign that says something like, "Don't be fooled. You're not down yet. Steep grades and tight curves ahead."

For days afterward, the newness of the loss and the myriad of follow-up duties provided a mild anesthesia that helped us keep moving. Then we came home and life resumed—without him. For my brother's wife, sons, and local family, even daily routines were immediately affected. For the rest of us across the country, not much changed in the practical outworking of our daily lives—except the profound and odd awareness that he was no longer with us.

It's difficult to describe how much that fact alone—the fact of a person's absence—can impact those who remain. Familiar tasks feel different for a while because now the world in which they are performed is a different world. We become strangely conscious of the routine—of almost everything, actually—not because the routine has changed but because we and our world have changed. So, we make calculations for navigating the rest of life; and we perform those calculations each day as if for the first time, attempting to inch our way a bit further along the rock face, not sure what's ahead or where the terrain will flatten.

I returned to work, grateful for the distraction of daily, predictable tasks, yet curious what the coming days would be like. As those days arrived and passed, I experienced some of what I expected: tears, sadness, and disbelief, often at random and unexpected times. Those emotions were punctuated, however, by other thoughts and feelings that I never could have anticipated.

As a rather introspective sort of person, I have often projected myself into this type of loss and recoiled at the thought of such loss. What I never could have anticipated were the strange forms of impact that this type of loss can have. Oh sure, there were some rather predictable emotional effects like loss of energy. For weeks I would sleep well, awake refreshed, go to work feeling rather normal, and be emotionally spent by lunch time. Day after day it was all I could do to go back to my desk and keep working until it was time to go home. This was tough, but understandable.

Often the ripple effects of grief do not feel like grief, but they are certainly related to it. There is no way I could have known that so many aspects of my own life and my sense of place in the world were linked to my brother's very existence, even though I only saw him or spoke to him by phone two or three times a year. In one sense, very little has changed in my day-to-day life. In another sense, everything in my life has been marked.

When someone you love chooses to die, life still goes on; but it goes on quite differently. Some of those differences are overt; many are subtle. And different types of responses and adjustments are necessary. On August 23, 2011 (three months after my brother's death) the Washington Monument was jarred by an earthquake of 5.8 magnitude. Subsequent repairs to the Monument included filling cracks, sealing leaks, and removing and replacing pieces of marble. In some places, however, the marble blocks had shifted approximately ¾ inch at the seams and nothing could be done about it, short of dismantling and rebuilding the structure from those points upward. So, the engineers decided to leave those shifted blocks alone, knowing that the overall compressed weight of the Monument offsets the asymmetry of those stressed seams.

The damage of a wrenching experience becomes part of the character of those who suffer it. In no way is that intended to romanticize the unthinkable. It is to point out that even though the damage cannot be undone, it does not have the last word. We can still live—with our wounds and limps and tears and grief, yes—but live gratefully and well nonetheless. Choosing to live after someone you love chooses to die does not happen naturally or easily. To move forward into that living takes thoughtful attention to little oddities unobservable from a distance, like hairline cracks in the monument. It takes the willingness to receive grace in tiny, unexpected doses; that is, to let God fill those cracks in His own time and manner. Sometimes we don't even know God is filling them. Then, one day we wake up and realize we're not cold and wet anymore.

2

Mars

Today as I write, the Mars Rover landed and is broadcasting back the first pictures of the red planet. Scientists will study those photos for years. Quite likely, by advancing our knowledge of what C.S. Lewis called "Thulcandra" they will enrich our understanding of our own planet. Yet few, if any, of us will ever actually have the opportunity to navigate that barren landscape. If we do, I'm certain that the photographs will only minimally prepare us for the actual experience.

Losing someone you love to suicide can be imagined and described in multiple ways. Yet, actually being present on such alien terrain brings emotions that you could not have predicted. Some of those emotions are so utterly foreign that it feels like being on another planet. By no means have I fully mapped the terrain, but perhaps I can provide a few points of orientation on this strange and daunting landscape. There is strength to be found in simply knowing that someone else has already been there and survived.

Hidden Losses

Some years ago I tore a muscle in my leg in such a way that it was beyond surgical repair. I made the foolish and arrogant mistake of trying to run a footrace against two fourteen-year-old boys at my youngest son's birthday party. Not only did I not stretch before running, but after years of not running regularly, I had lost a measure of muscular flexibility without knowing it. On that occasion I subjected myself to a physical test that exposed what I had lost.

It takes a while after an unthinkable loss to realize how much was actually lost. Most obvious, of course, is the person who died. We lose the opportunity for presence and interaction. We lose the subtle, easily taken for granted (sometimes delightful, sometimes exasperating) parts of our lives made up of how that person did things. How he hung his clothes. How she commented on TV programs. Idiosyncracies. Sights, sounds, and smells remind us of an environment that at the time seemed ordinary and mundane, yet now bursts with meaning because a person who was so integral to that environment is gone (and chose to leave!). That's one type of loss. But there are more, less obvious losses.

Along the way I realized that when my brother took his own life, he took part of mine, too. Though we were several years apart in age, lived many miles apart, only saw each other and talked occasionally, he was much more a part of me than I ever realized. When he took his own life he took part of me with him. He changed my future because now it will not involve seeing him or hearing his voice on the phone. He took from me energy I need to engage my own responsibilities and ongoing relationships in a robust manner. He took from me a measure of my own happiness and replaced it with a thick, slow current of sadness that now flows slowly, often quietly, under even my many good days.

All this may sound like pathetic self-pity, I know. Admittedly, I've stated these things like a helpless victim. I don't really believe I'm helpless, but I needed to describe the matter that way. While I don't have to adopt a victim mentality, I can still honestly admit to being a victim. I did not ask for this, did not deserve it, and I don't know of anything I could have done to prevent it. For those of us who remain behind such tragedies, our lives have been permanently altered— even disfigured in some sense. Whatever led my brother to take his own life (and I'll deal with that more sympathetically later), he had no right to do this to any of us. He may have had reasons, but he had no right! And I need to be able to say that if I'm genuinely to forgive and heal. I feel robbed!

I've been shocked to realize how much of my identity was tied to my relationship with my brother, even though we were not regular participants in each other's lives. For him to leave jars my sense of place in the world. I am now one of only three siblings, not four. I am now the only boy among my siblings (even though now in my late 50s, I still think of myself as a boy in our family). It feels strangely lonely. There is a huge hole in my psyche. I don't think this is unhealthy; it simply reflects the fact that our sense of identity is more defined by others than we might realize—particularly in more individualistic Western cultures.

Hidden Heartbreak

With my anger and complex sense of loss out on the table, I can now talk more honestly about how my heart is wrenched for the sense of despair and hopelessness that must have led my brother to end his life. Even when a person leaves a note behind, we still can know only a few surface layers of what really transpired inside that person. We may know some of the circumstances, but we may never fully know the convoluted internal turmoil—what it felt like to BE him or her.

What hurts me just as deeply as my losses is the knowledge that his fatal end was probably in the making for some time in order for it to culminate in the act. Perhaps it began just as a fleeting thought but as the contributing factors intensified it became a more viable option. Along the way, did he fully consider the effects it would have on others? If so, did that merely compound his miserable sense of helplessness? He must have been slowly dying internally long before he died physically.

I look at a picture hanging on the wall of my study. It's of the two of us having a great time when last we saw each other a year and a half prior to his death. What was going on for him when that picture was taken? Was he at that time making decisions or experiencing struggles that would slowly culminate this way? I wish I had known. I wish our conversation had turned in such a direction that he would have felt some impulse and safety to share his pain with me. He seemed so strong, so resilient, up to any challenge. I'm crushed to know that someone I loved so much was suffering in his spirit to the extent that he felt vanquished. These thoughts add to my heartbreak.

Such multi-layered grief and multi-faceted losses cause us to redefine the life of the one we loved. It's not merely a matter of how we remember them; it's also how we understand their lives on this side of their deaths. How do I feel about one who crumbled under privately borne pressures that he felt he could not share without doing greater damage? How do I put together in my own mind the irreconcilable elements of his situation? What do I do with the unknown and disjointed factors? How am I to understand all this and honor it without ignoring, trivializing, diluting it? How can I now view his life so that his physical end does not define, over-shadow, or nullify the good in his life and the blessedness that we experienced from him?

Who is he to me (and to my family) now? We not only have to redefine *him*, but also ourselves. Who are we and who am I without him? Who am I as one to whom this type of tragedy actually could or did happen? Without realizing it, a significant part of my previous identity was shaped by the fact that something like this had *not* happened to me. Now it *has* happened—and I'm not the same person anymore. I knew, theoretically and statistically—even theologically—that this type of thing *could* happen to me. And it was not that I honestly thought it never *would*. It's simply that apart from it, I could not see myself that way because I can only imagine so much. When we try to imagine such things, we can then easily leave those thoughts behind because they are not real. When they are no longer mere thoughts but history, we have been changed. It will never not have happened.

Senses and Insensibilities

In the days immediately after we received the news of Bob's death, I wanted coffee more than ever. I'm truly not a coffee-addict (though I drink more of it than I should). But I craved a big cup of really good coffee—the kind you generally have to buy at an upscale coffee house.

It was probably three days after his death before I had a chance to find my way to the nearest coffee shop. That morning had been intensely difficult for me as I had struggled to put together a sermon for his upcoming funeral service. I resisted the task and found all kinds of distractions to keep from getting to it. Finally, I finished it and hopped in my truck to go somewhere and satisfy that craving.

I ordered the biggest vanilla latte on the menu. The sky was bright and clear that day. The air was just crisp enough and just warm enough to stimulate pleasant sensations on the skin. So, I took the coffee to my truck, parked overlooking a lake, rolled down the windows and sat there for an hour savoring it—musing—praying. My tactile memory is loaded from that one hour. Everything else that I was experiencing was still so surreal that I was disoriented—feeling out of sync with the universe, as if I was there but not there, all at the same time. That coffee tasted just like many other vanilla lattes that I have consumed. But against that backdrop, the taste of THAT latte lingers to this day.

Days of constant thirst for that cup of coffee made me realize that the pain of loss has a couple of side effects. First, and somewhat predictably, experiencing an unthinkable loss creates a sort of numbness and emptiness—a deadness that drains much of our capacity for responsiveness to the routine pleasures and challenges of life. For a frighteningly indefinite time, we can lose interest in tasks, hobbies, conversations, humor, and other matters that we normally would find engaging. It can take all we have simply to tackle routine responsibilities. What we normally would find intriguing and inviting becomes one-dimensional and bland.

Second, the loss can heighten some of our other senses. This may feel paradoxical. Perhaps this is analogous to the way those who lose their sight or hearing experience compensation with their other senses. Small, ordinary pleasures take on an intensified significance, whether it's the feel of fresh air and sunshine or the taste of coffee. Somehow these sensations, deadening emptiness and the acute hungers, feed off each other. I understand how people can turn to substance abuse and develop addictions as a result of trauma. I wanted anything at all that would make me feel good in any way, help alleviate the pain, provide some sense of relief, even if temporarily.

As the weeks passed, I noticed other appetites surfacing in an unusual and distracting manner. I have to believe those were different versions of that intense desire for coffee. Most of us, I suspect, have certain default impulses to which we gravitate for a sense of relief when we're under stress or in pain. Whether those impulses are shopping, drugs, sexual activity, or even obsessive/compulsive actions, we're looking for immediate relief. I noticed a recurring fascination with getting a sports car or a motorcycle—something fast—anything that felt good and distracting at a visceral level!

These understandable impulses easily lead to addictions and other disorders that leave us vulnerable to even more crippling forms of bondage. Toxins take many forms, from chemical substances to coping mechanisms. They slip into our lives and handcuff us through our longing to alleviate pain or fill a gap in our lives. As fallen and sinful as I already am, I realized how much more vulnerable I am to even further deviation from the person God made me to be.

So I came up with a fancy name for this syndrome (having a name for something always seems to give a sense of control over it). I call it my V-I Index, which stands for "Vulnerability-Impulse Index." Under the stress and drain of grief, we become more susceptible to particular temptations. If we know what our default impulses are even when life is reasonably normal, we have some sense of what to watch out for when pain and loss strike. We are then better able not to take those impulses quite so seriously and not believe what they tell us, which is generally something like, "This will actually make the pain go away, or meet my need, or make a difference in my situation."

Knowing my V-I Index allows me to understand a bit of what's happening when my impulses are going crazy. Then, I can better identify healthy ways to stop the drain and fill the emptiness that intensified the vulnerability in the first place. For me that vanilla latte was a pretty safe "fix" and the hour enjoying it by the lake was a gift from God. But it could have been a short hop from that to more disastrous "remedies."

This has taught me something about how to pray in times when pain is intense or deadening and when I want anything that will help me feel good. In those times I need to verbalize to God what I'm feeling (the Psalmists certainly did that!) and consciously give that numbness or pain to Him. I have to say to God things like, "Somehow, because of Jesus, you know what I'm feeling right now. He conquered this so it doesn't own me, but I really need your Spirit to make that real to me. I'll trust you to do that, but I need help—badly—and soon." I've prayed prayers of that sort lots of times since Bob's death. Having prayed that, I might just go get another latte.

Fear

For months after Bob's death something cringed inside me every time my cell phone vibrated. That fateful call on May 10 created some visceral connections inside me. Irrational? Yes. But where is the switch to turn off such paranoia? Who's next? When is the next blow going to knock me down? Will I ever get up if I take another blow like this? Those questions kept coming like a steady facet drip.

After a few months my cell phone no longer had that effect, at least not as often or as predictably. Yet, I noticed that the fear had seeped underneath my emotional topsoil. I had slowly developed something of a fear-based approach to life in general. I must admit that from childhood I have had some of those tendencies, so this is not entirely new. But my brother's death got into my emotional groundwater, reactivated some of those fearful defaults from my past, and brought them back to the surface after having dealt with and "conquered" many of them.

These fears were not crippling. I never experienced agoraphobia or other paralyzing sensations. But certain compulsions returned: compulsive thoughts and terrors that had not really bothered me in years. Psychologists would tell me, I expect, that those compulsions are ways of attempting to cope with fear, bring a sense of equilibrium or symmetry to the world. That would ring true for me! My world has been knocked off its axis. At random and unexpected times my interior world feels like a washing machine trying to spin an unbalanced load of clothes. You know what that sounds like!

How have I dealt with those fears? Well, as far as the compulsive fears go, a bit of reading on obsessive-compulsive disorder (OCD) has reassured me that I'm probably not crazy. It has given me some helpful ideas for reprogramming my defaults when those fears randomly drop in for a visit. Writing some of this in a journal has helped. My prayers have changed in a more positive direction, trusting God with my brokenness and seeking His grace for whatever underlies these fears. I'm treating this as an occasion to push deeper into God's healing grace, especially in ways that I didn't realize I needed grace prior to the tragedy.

As for the paranoia, the visceral recoil when my phone buzzes or the subtle expectation that something else is about to go wrong, some of that has faded—very slowly, but it has faded. Telling a mentor and some close friends about this has helped. It defuses some of the fear by bringing it into the light. Words have a strange way of giving us a measure of control, handles for things that otherwise have us in their grip.

In the maze of fears was also the periodic question about whether something is wrong with our family. Do we have some genetic, psychological irregularity or vulnerability that might subject others of us to self-destruction? Whether from nature or nurture, do we have some type of susceptibility in our family blind spot?

What are we missing about ourselves? What does this indicate about not merely my brother, but about the rest of us? These questions can circulate through the minds of survivors, adding thin but burdensome layers to the experience.

This is going to be a long journey.

Angry Grieving

Let me return to the theme of being robbed. How do I feel OK about being angry (dare I say "mad as Hell"?) at someone I miss so badly? Someone for whom my heart sags with a heavy sadness just thinking about what his inner world must have been like . . . perhaps for a long time . . . to lead him to the point of self-destruction? It's a bizarre and scrambled knot of emotions—a knot tied with countless complex and random loops, then pulled together so tightly that the different threads are barely distinguishable.

For the sake of discretion and my brother's honor, I won't restate the things I said to him when I first saw his casket (yes, even as a theologian who knows better, I was talking to my dead brother—emotions sometimes burst right through one's theological scruples!). Nor will I repeat the things some of our family members said. Those words were both furious and sacred. You can probably guess some of them.

What does it look like or feel like to be simultaneously angry and grief-stricken? What does it mean to forgive when there is no way to have a conversation with the offender? How does one forgive when the victim and the perpetrator are the same person? These emotional puzzles stared back at me frequently, daring me to attempt a neat, rational resolution.

Obviously, I was not inside my brother's head and can't know how tangled life looked to him or the sense of desperation that led him to this act. But I'm still angry at him for not letting anyone get close enough to help him. I'm angry at him for the decisions he made all along the way—large and small—that consummated in this act. I'm angry at him for the irreversible effects this has had and will continue to have on so many people. Yet, I know that none of us are immune from decisions of that same character, whether or not we take it that far.

After all, how do the character of his decision and his feeling of desperation differ from my own periodic desperation? Only by degree, I suspect. Do I have a right to my anger with him? I think I do. Does my anger place me on a moral high ground where I can sit in judgment on him? I think not. Does forgiveness make my anger go away, never to return? I'm not sure about that right now, but expect that I'll move back and forth between anger and forgiveness for a long time.

So, while my family and I must find a way to forgive him for what he has done, I suppose he may have to forgive us (whatever that means and looks like theologically—and don't ask me to defend the theology behind that one!) for our anger at him and the things we (I) have said about him and said to him since his death. What do we do with the anger and other convoluted emotions when the effects of the act left incalculable scars and messes for others who have now been victimized by the victim?

While I'm on the subject of anger, what about anger with God? Over the past few years it has become increasingly safe to talk about being angry with God. Sometimes I wonder whether it's now even fashionable or hip to be mad at God! Make no mistake; I've been furious at God any number of times in my life, and usually for fairly petty reasons—at least for reasons much less severe than a loved one's suicide. So, I'll not assume the moral high ground here.

On this one occasion, however, it surprised me that I never got angry with God. I hope that's an indicator of a maturing and more richly textured faith, but we'll see how that holds up with future losses. At any rate, this time I experienced none of that, and a few times I wondered whether I should have. Was I in denial? Certainly, I am as perplexed and mystified as ever at God. I'm challenged and stretched in my trust of God who declares himself faithful (and I still believe he is) but is not predictable for specific outcomes in this life. So, my trust in God has most definitely been stretched even if I did not get angry at God.

I did, however, become intensely mad at the evil and sin in the world that somehow got hold of my brother. That evil may have been direct, in the form of his personal decisions, or it may have been indirect, the cumulative effects of sin in a broken world where people can be led to despair for inscrutable reasons. It was probably both, but it really doesn't matter. It was all evil. And there is an Evil One behind it all. I'm stunned at how insidious and subtle are the effects of evil in the world, destroying us while we become numb to what is taking place, bringing us to places of despair and destruction. And I'm mad at that! I wish I hated sin and evil that much when it is MY sin, but that's another subject.

Other Emotional Oddities

Anger and grief were no surprise to me. Having dealt with lots of people who have suffered the tragic loss of someone they love, I was not blindsided by the assault of the emotions or by their intensity. I was not surprised by the alternating and sometimes tangled arrangement of those emotions. Plenty of books have been written describing and validating those parallel lanes of anger and grief on this journey.

The most common adjective I have used to describe the aftermath of dealing with my brother's death is "weird." It's a packaged experience that contains some of the most unexpected and strange emotions. At times it's strange because I feel things that I would not label as grief, yet I know they are the ripple effects of the grief; all connected somehow. At some point in the past I have probably told others that there is no script for how one is supposed to feel when grieving a tragic loss. I knew that feelings are complex and unpredictable. Now I am discovering personally just how complex and unpredictable—how utterly *strange* those feelings really are! For starters, I realized that I now think about my brother almost every day and did not do so while he was alive. I don't really feel guilty about that—just odd!

The odd sensations continue when the emotions don't come in linear fashion. I don't seem to be making progress in a straight line from one stage of grief to another. I loop back and forth through different emotions after I thought I might be mostly done with a phase. At least I had the benefit of some categories and language for these phases. That's the advantage of receiving training as a pastor or caregiver.

However, professional training alone can leave a person with the impression that the real experience unfolds sort of like a textbook unfolds—one page at a time. If you *want* to flip back and reread a section you can do so, but it's entirely at your discretion as the reader. You don't expect to read along and find a chapter that you already read reappearing later in the book. That would indicate either a publication mistake or an insane author. So, when the experience of grief unfolds that way, it can knock you back a bit. For example, what sense does it make to be angry, to forgive, then be angry all over again—perhaps even more intensely than you were at first?

Another bizarre phenomenon occurs when random and insignificant events evoke a deep and undefined sadness that does not feel directly related to the person who died. Even when I am feeling relatively normal and past the immediate pain of my loss, I realize that my emotions are never very far below the surface and can be triggered quite easily.

A deep current of sadness now runs underneath all my emotions. Often I'm not aware of it and I feel fine—even happy! And that happiness is not merely superficial or cheap. It's simply that a deeper, slower, denser undercurrent has been dug out underneath it. And it doesn't take very much to penetrate through to those dark, murky waters down below. It's strange how quickly and unexpectedly I can move from feeling normal and happy to feeling a profound sadness; not always consciously sad about my brother— simply sad.

Sometimes I don't feel anything at all for my brother or I feel really good and then feel strange (or guilty) for feeling so. Rather soon after his death, I remember feeling numb toward him. That's not too surprising, I suppose. After all, the wrenching emotional intensity of those first days sapped me. I was amazed at how many tears I could cry and even began to wonder whether I would dehy-drate from crying so much! Numbness is to be expected. But it did not feel right to feel numb—to feel nothing. This was my brother, for crying out loud! What kind of cold-hearted, messed up person feels nothing so soon after such a loss? Those are the thoughts that swam around in my head.

Any counselor or psychologist with even modest training will read what I have just written and be able to offer a tidy explana-tion or diagnosis. I may not have all the technical language at my disposal, but I think I could offer a pretty satisfactory diagnosis of my own experience. But being able to do this does not negate the need to say it. We labor under a grand and horrible illusion if we think that we can bypass the pain or effects of these experiences simply by having categories to explain them. Not so! They need to be stated, just as if the diagnoses were not there at all.

Another oddity, at least it may sound strange, is that grieving people need to laugh and party—even in the early stages. Some may think that is superficial or a symptom of denial (and perhaps for some it is). But laughter and celebration do not necessarily ig-nore the brutal reality of a loss. In fact, they provide an emotional counterweight and prophetic indictment of the loss. There must be times when we can cut loose and celebrate life, even with all its pain and loss.

The first party I attended after Bob's death was with some of my closest friends. I was eager to laugh and reconnect with some-thing in life that was positive, normal, unchanged, and healthy. Another surprise—when I got to the party I found it difficult to really enjoy it, which surprised and disappointed me. Months later I've concluded that that was OK. I still needed to be there. I needed to be around other happy people, even though they were feeling sorry for me and somewhat awkward about my situation.

What might look like denial or superficiality to some is actu-ally emotional survival. In the middle of and peppered throughout our family's tears and grieving was a lot of joking and laughing. Was it inappropriate or oddly placed? It felt odd but it did not feel inappropriate. It reflected a limited capacity to stay in the depths of emotional pain. We needed to come up for air. Laughter indicates a greater reality and hope that encompasses even our most intense grief. As a Christian, it's a subtle way of refusing death and loss the final word. Through laughter we express defiance against what threatens to own and control our lives. Through laughter we can express our faith in God.

Mars Again

I can't actually imagine myself on Mars in any way that comes close to really being there! Annually, some friends and I hike in the rugged plains of Wyoming. When I stand on a mesa and look out over vast acreage, it looks primarily flat and benign. Then I cross that stretch of land and discover all kinds of gullies and berms that were visually flattened from my elevated vantage point. You can hardly walk without stepping in or over cactus. You can easily turn your ankle in snake dens.

The terrain of this loss has a lot more irregularities than I expected. Lots of places don't look all that menacing from afar, but once you set foot on them you can lose your way or worse. I'm beginning to feel that perhaps I have been to Mars after all.

3

New

IN THE AFTERMATH OF a suicide (or any wrenching loss for that matter), finding hope is essential. However, the quest for hope can involve dead-ends and tempting detours because we desperately want to feel better, to live as if it never happened. We want to find assurance of insulation from future losses. So, we seek hope from sources that cannot deliver. We may try to control those we love, assuming we can protect them. We may live in anger and bitterness, assuming that we can have the final word with God and subtly get even with him for letting us experience tragedy. We may turn up the intensity of our spiritual practices, seeking to atone for prior spiritual laziness or in hopes that God will reward us by not letting such things happen again.

These and other responses may have a measure of validity. After all, it's good to exercise healthy precautions, be honest with our anger, and be more spiritually attentive. Yet, each of these can be deceptive and addictive, actually working against genuine hope in our lives. So, what does honest, realistic hope look like and where is it to be found?

Of course, Scripture clearly tells us that in Christ our hope is already secured for the eternal future. We can experience this hope as a reality now because of the Holy Spirit's presence in our lives, even though we still look forward to its culmination. Throughout Scripture we see God's people living in that bittersweet present-future tension. We have already tasted what we anticipate, but the anticipation still involves a painful longing. In the case of a crushing, senseless, and irreversible loss (such as a suicide), authentic hope will have a gritty texture. Hope does not reverse our losses or make it as if a tragedy never happened. Things are not reversed; they are different.

We are given hope when God promises to do something new. Ezra 9:9 records God giving his enslaved people new life to rebuild the Temple. Isaiah 42:9 states God's promise to bring about new conditions of liberation from bondage and to restore his people to usefulness. In Ephesians 4:23 Paul points out how Christ creates newness in our minds.

This pair of themes—newness and hope—punctuates the entire Christian faith journey! This newness is fresh and life-giving, not because it masks the past but because it stands against the backdrop of the past. The enslavement, the ruins, the distortions, and the losses still reside in the memory banks. The grooves they have cut in our lives don't get filled. Rather, they become the contours that hope follows. That's what makes hope gritty, textured, and deeply real.

Let's get more specific, though. How does God actually make things new? What does that sense of newness look like? If we cannot manipulate or manufacture that hope, how do we at least open ourselves to it as God's gift on God's terms? Two key themes come into view and lead us forward: redemption and forgiveness.

Redemption

Redemption is a hot topic in film, literature, and therapy, as well as in theological discussions. The word is almost cliché by now. When any word becomes commonplace it ends up with different meanings to different people. Even theologians use the word *redemption* in different ways. God's promise of redemption in Scripture affords priceless hope and perspective. However, that redemption does not provide us with a shortcut around facing the pain and ugliness of losses like those involved with suicide.

Make no mistake. I firmly believe, and still teach, that God can redeem anything. No experience is a complete or final loss when it is given to God. That is, God can turn any loss on its head, without reversing it or making it as if it never happened. Instead, he robs it of defining power over us. I believe this to be true now more than ever, even though my experience of that is gradual with regard to my brother's suicide.

For most of my life I have heard Christians speak about experiencing God's presence in the midst of horrible loss and pain. I have often wondered what that felt like, never understanding exactly what it meant. In the days immediately following Bob's death, I thought about this quite a bit. During the times of our most intense grief, I wondered what I was supposed to be feeling that would signal the presence of God. I'm still pondering this because I don't think I hurt any less or cried any less than I would have otherwise.

Does redemption mean that out of this tragedy some good will emerge that counterbalances or offsets the loss? Good of some sort may indeed come about, but that will not make the loss OK. When we try to quantify and compare good and evil in that manner, we inevitably trivialize the horror of losses and we foster images of God that are both unbiblical and faith-crippling. No. Loss, tragedy, and benefit cannot be quantified in that manner.

I have no doubt that God works *in* all things to bring about His good purposes for His people (Romans 8:28). Regardless of how thoughtlessly and sometimes cruelly this passage of Scripture is thrown around, I still believe it. And I'm glad when I hear that God has redemptively used a tragedy to get the attention of people whose lives were hurdling toward destruction (or perhaps even prompts people to write books that might comfort others). Who would not be grateful that some good could come out of something truly bad? Let me be honest, though. At this point in my life I cannot imagine anything coming out of my brother's death that will make it "OK" or that will make me pain-free for the rest of my life. I will be grateful for any good that comes from it, but the scales don't work that way. It will never be OK that he took his life.

It will never not matter. Those of us who walk this path have to be able to say that in order for redemptive newness to have honesty and substance.

What I can affirm is a sense of being upheld by God, even if I was more aware of it after the fact. Perhaps the most discernible difference is being able to turn to God and trust God right in the middle of the most intense times of grief. That is all rather subjective, but it's no less real. God's presence is not always a sensation that we feel or one that we feel in a predictable manner. Just read through the Psalms and you will find repeated descriptions of a sense of abandonment during times of trouble. All but a very few (like Psalm 88) express some type of resolution or trust in God. And maybe that Psalm is there as a subtle reminder that we don't always have to have a neat and tidy bow tacked onto the end of a grief episode in order for God to be upholding us through it all.

The full redemption of this loss still lies ahead. I await it with no idea of either what it will look like or how much of it may occur in my lifetime. God's promise that in Christ all things will be reconciled means more to me than ever. I have a lot more weight resting on that promise now. God's promise to wipe away every tear and make all things new has an almost visceral impact on me every time I read it. But I must tell you about one particular installment of redemption.

As I approached the first anniversary of Bob's death I did not know what to expect, except that it might be a difficult day. Fortunately, I had the luxury of not going to work that day. I only wanted to be alone, with the freedom to reflect, pray, cry, or whatever I needed to do and feel.

The day began rather uneventfully with a good, long workout. As I left the gym and got in my car, a brief but subtle wave of emotion hit me as I realized that almost right at that very time of day one year ago, my brother was ending his life. It was still emotionally stretching to consider and absorb that fact. I spent the day roaming around in a relaxed manner, not doing much of anything.

Late in the afternoon I decided to drive to another city about 45 minutes away to shop for a new gadget I had been wanting. It seemed like a harmless and pleasant diversion. As I drove up the interstate I noticed a store that I thought sold what I wanted, so I quickly took the next exit. Turning right, I suddenly noticed that I was driving past a cemetery, a sight that on any other day would have meant nothing to me. On that day, however, it quickly opened a torrent of memories.

One block later I took another right turn to get to the store and found myself driving past the funeral home. That unfolded another layer of memory. Strange, but perhaps just coincidental, I thought, that I'm encountering these images on this day. It hit me quite fleetingly at that moment that these were the same images from a year ago, yet they were not the same cemetery or funeral home. They were different—new images.

After shopping for perhaps half an hour, I got back on the highway, but quickly decided that what I REALLY wanted was an exceptionally good cup of coffee. I remembered how badly I wanted that in the days immediately after his death, when anything in the least bit pleasurable was so inviting. Though by this time I was across the city from where I live, I seemed to remember that there was some good coffee somewhere along the next major cross street. So, I took the next exit.

Less than a mile down that street, while looking for coffee, I noticed a crematorium office. That's odd, I thought. Never expected that. Bob was cremated and this image added to the growing irony of the past hour. Then, only a few blocks further, I saw a coffee shop. Paydirt—that's what I want! The very next instant I saw a restaurant right next to it. And it was one of the same chain of restaurants that we had just entered one year earlier when that fateful call came through from my sister. This was getting a bit strange.

I turned into the parking lot, entered the coffee shop and, just as I had done a year earlier, ordered the biggest vanilla latte they offered. With Bible, journal, and latte in hand, I sat down looking through the window and across the lane at the restaurant, pondering the significance of this. Not long after I sat down I received a text message from a man I don't really know that well. A few years ago I got on a list of people to whom he sends a daily Scripture by text message. The texts show up at different times each day, but that day it arrived at that ironic juncture. Though he knew nothing of my situation, the Scripture passage he texted to me that day was Jeremiah 29:11.

> "For I know the plans I have for you, declares the Lord, plans for wholeness and not for evil, to give you a future and a hope."

"Wow, that's timely," I thought.

A few moments later, while I sat there staring at the restaurant through the window, pondering all that was taking place, another text message arrived, this one from my oldest son. He simply said that he was praying for me, then listed Zephaniah 3:17. I had to look that one up. Here's what I found.

> "The Lord your God is in your midst, a mighty one who will save; he will rejoice over you with gladness; he will quiet you by his love; he will exult over you with loud singing."

Something was happening inside me. God was tending to me in an uncanny fashion.

Realizing that that moment was within an hour of the time one year ago when I received that horrible phone call, I was struck by how God had brought so many images of the previous year back across my path; eerily familiar, yet different. While each evoked painful memories, each also had something new about it. God was not discarding those memories and putting the pain behind me. He was giving them back to me in a new way. This set of images bore his fingerprints. God was somehow present to me in them.

Sitting there musing on all this in the coffee shop, I decided to take a step I had been considering for most of the previous year. As friends found out about Bob's death, many of them had quickly sent text messages of prayer and loving support. I had saved and treasured all those messages for the entire year. They were sacred to me. I opened my cell phone and reread each message, savoring the persons and the concern behind them. Then, though with mixed feelings . . . I deleted them, one by one. With this move I closed a chapter and at least grabbed the edge of the page to begin a new one.

The experience brought no expectations that all the pain would go away. I have still cried since then. I harbored no illusions that the grief had been completed. I'll grieve my brother and miss him for the rest of my life, perhaps even more at some points when I realize how long it has been since I saw him, heard his voice, heard my own voice in his voice, laughed with him, hugged him. But something was different for me. Finishing my latte, closing my phone, journal, and Bible, getting in my car to head home, I knew that God had met me.

What does it mean to experience God's redemption of such a loss? Since "redemption" can be used in multiple senses, we must be clear on what we expect. Redemption is not necessarily the reversal of an event, whether it's something we did or something we experienced. Though we would give almost anything for that, events don't "unhappen." Nor is redemption the equalizing of the loss with some good that supposedly counterbalances the loss. This may sound frighteningly unholy, but though I may thank God for how he uses a tragic loss, that does not make me glad it happened. It would not prompt me to choose that loss if I had such a choice. I prefer that God bring about that good in another way. I don't know *why* things happen the way they do. Nobody knows that, even though some claim to know and it brings a sensation of comfort to think we (or someone else) knows what God is up to. God has not opened the curtain to that back room for anyone as far as I know (he did not even open it for Job!).

At the very least, redemption involves the transformation of an experience, even if gradually, into something different than it would be by itself; something different because God has touched it, so to speak. When we begin to see that God is still present to us, upholding us, caring for us, somehow defining us in our loss, somehow touching our loss so that it no longer has the last word on our lives, we are experiencing redemption.

Something redemptive occurs when we become more deeply human, more attentive to others, more sensitive to the learning that is embedded in suffering. I have to reemphasize that this is not some cheap, mathematical balancing of the scales. It's simply refusing to allow suffering to be wasted or to be lost on us. In this sense redemption does not come to us glibly or easily. We can easily miss God's redemptive work, ignore it, resist it, let it slide off us. Redemption can even have its own unique pain—a holy pain—in which hurting and healing feel quite similar.

Several years ago I planned to paint the concrete floor of my garage until I learned that much more was involved than simply washing and painting it. I discovered that even after a thorough cleaning you have to spread an acidic solution on the concrete for a day or so to "etch" the surface. This etching adds texture to the concrete so that the paint will stick. Suffering can do this for us— "etch" our lives with a texture that was not there previously and that now can be either add an abrasive or an adhesive quality to our lives. I pray for the latter.

Experiencing some newness or hope through redemption means growing in our capacity for gratitude. I don't mean becoming grateful that a horrible event like a suicide occurred. I honestly don't expect that I will or ever should be grateful that my brother took his own life. Nor am I saying we should merely focus on the good things about his life in hopes that those memories will somehow outweigh the bad ending. As I suggested above, trying to quantify the good and the bad in any person's life is, in general, a futile and forced exercise. While some circumstances may lend themselves to such rationalizing, many do not. They are far too complex. Rather, gratitude means opening our hearts to God as the One who enters the depths of that suffering with us, as One who knows our suffering from the inside—through Jesus—and not from a safe distance. *The cultivation of gratitude is the difference between grief and despair. It's what allows us to grieve genuinely without imploding.*

We can receive the gift of our loved one's life as a gift to be celebrated. Death cannot suffocate gratitude. It has no power over gratitude. We can refuse to let death erode or eclipse the reality of the love we shared with person. Death cannot erase love. We can receive and choose to live on God's promise that in Jesus He has conquered death and robbed it of its final power to define either this life or the next. Death does not own us.

As I stood by my brother's casket for the internment service, I read Paul's defiant declaration against death in 1 Corinthians 15. I have read those words countless times in my life. I have read them numerous times while standing at the gravesides of others, many of whom I did not know personally. It was quite strange to read them on that day as I drew on every ounce of nerve I could find just to speak through my own tears. But I read them with the same defiance that I sense was in Paul's heart; it was a holy, strangely grateful defiance!

It turns out that gratitude has far more facets under the microscope than I can see with my naked eye. A loss such as what I experienced serves to magnify those subtleties. I have an expanded capacity for gratitude in the moments of my life; for the love I can give and receive; for quickly passing sunsets; for fresh, cool air on a summer morning; for the warmth and taste of a meal; for good work to do.

It's not that I never previously thought those things or felt grateful for them and many other intricate features of life. I did—often. Yet, something is different—new. They mean more to me now, perhaps because they are both so good and so fleeting, whispering of the timeless and mystery nature of God's goodness. This expanded capacity allows me to ask the big *why* question about those little graces (not merely about my losses), realizing more and more that, by definition, they are intrinsically gratuitous.

Admittedly, I've often struggled with the question of why God seems to exercise that wonderful redeeming power *after* so many tragedies and does not do so to prevent them. That question will probably haunt me on and off for the rest of my life. If I ever have a chance to put that question to God, I may get the same type of response that Job received when he had his day in court. I have provisionally concluded that I will never understand the calculus of redemption. In all honesty, that's the source of my doubts and frustrations; I want an accounting—a calculus, of sorts—for *why* and *how* God is involved and not involved in the affairs of this life. Perhaps I'll never get an explanation, even in the new heavens and new earth. But I do hang onto that hope for a new heavens and earth—for the redemption of all things even if not the understanding of all things. I'm beginning to believe that redemption does not equal understanding.

Whatever redemption means, it always involves something new. The new does not have to eclipse the old or trivialize it or make it as if it never happened. Even though Job got a new family and a restored fortune, I'm sure he hurt for the balance of his life from the hole left by the loss of his first family. The *new* of redemption moves us forward knowing that God has met us and is moving us forward. God is present and at work. God is Lord over pain and loss. I try to hang onto that. More importantly, that hangs onto me.

Forgiveness

So, what about forgiveness? Earlier I mentioned the struggle involved in simultaneously experiencing grief and anger, stemming from my brother being both victim and perpetrator. How do I synchronize grieving him and forgiving him? How do I forgive him when the forgiveness cannot repair anything between us; cannot go any further to produce reconciliation or healing?

Forgiveness can be a complex process. The complexity must not dilute the force and clarity of God's command to forgive, so we must still choose at least to step into forgiveness. We take that step depending on God's grace to help us through the pain and confusion to figure out what it means to forgive. We need God's grace to forgive even before we can understand or explain it.

What do we do with our anger? Where do we put the wrong that was done, regardless of how heartbroken we are for whatever led to it? Forgiveness begins for me by acknowledging that, whatever may have crushed in on my brother, however sympathetic I may be to the unknowable horrors and desperation that he felt, however much I may grieve all that—*it was still wrong for him to take his life.* The grief I feel tempts me to soften that statement out of compassion. Admittedly, those emotions don't fit together neatly. Yet, genuine forgiveness is only possible when an act of wrongdoing is called what it is. There is in fact something to be forgiven.

Anger is proper in the face of evil and injustice. Suicide is all that, not *merely* that, but it is at least that. The person who commits suicide has done wrong. I hope that does not sound too harsh or unfeeling. It's actually the first and essential step toward forgiveness and healing. Otherwise, those of us left behind a suicide are likely to be angry anyway but never really deal with it because we feel guilty about being angry at our loved one.

An important step for me has been recognizing that genuine forgiveness depends on legitimate anger. Otherwise, it's terribly easy to get stuck at the crossroads of anger and forgiveness when they seem to be one-way streets headed in opposite directions. Those roads merge in a healthy direction when my anger exposes the substance of what I must forgive.

What about reconciliation? The type of forgiveness that must be exercised with a suicide forces an important distinction into view. Forgiveness and reconciliation are not synonymous. Reconciliation certainly depends on forgiveness, but forgiveness does not always lead to reconciliation. Forgiveness can take place unilaterally. Reconciliation, by definition, is a mutual process and can be even more complicated. I can forgive a person even when reconciliation is not possible.

Reconciliation involves both parties. They must be able to communicate and come to terms with what stands between them. Forgiveness must be offered, but it must also be received, based on acknowledgement of the need for it. In the case of suicide this type of interchange is not accessible to us. We live without the prospect of closure. If we're not careful, this fact can loop back into frustration and unresolved anger for survivors.

The word "unresolved" contains an important clue to our dilemma. We may not be able to reconcile with our loved one, but our anger can be resolved. At this point the powerful themes of anger, forgiveness, and reconciliation can merge into resolution.

Resolution *does not* erase my questions. It *does not* mean that I have answers to those wrenching questions. Resolution *does not* inoculate me against future grieving. Resolution *does* bring these perplexing and painful factors together in a new harmony whose overall direction is more powerful and evocative than the individual, discordant parts. Just as in a complex musical score, the dissonant features provide character to the piece.

Resolution, genuine resolution, I am convinced, leaves the reconciliation of all things to God (Col. 1:15-20, Rev. 21:3-5). Resolution lives in anticipation; it lives on the down payment of God's promise. A crude analogy that comes to my mind is that resolution is a bit like the feeling I have as I'm getting over a horrible bout of the flu. In this stage of recovery I'm not well yet. In fact, if I could snapshot the way I feel at a given moment, I still don't feel quite right. Yet, how I feel at that moment is connected to how I was feeling when the illness was at its worst. How I feel at that moment is part of a movie. It's not a still frame photo. So, with the worst having passed I can feel myself getting well. I can feel the wellness on its way even if the progress comes slowly and in tiny increments. I know I'm going to make it and that gives a different character to the isolated moments of discomfort.

My own journey with redemption and forgiveness in this loss is but a sliver of the newness that the Bible promises. It has charted a new course for me. It is a sort of preface to a new narrative in my life. What I experienced one year after Bob's death wrote a new chapter in that story. Other chapters may not be quite as satisfying or poignant. Still, I anticipate how God will continue to write the story. Whatever the particulars of the story will be, whatever pain or confusion I experience in the future, whatever ripple effects that I must face, this is God's story. I've tasted a little bit of redemption and forgiveness. As small as those bites may be, they are part of the real meal. Beyond that, I don't know much. And, frankly, I'm not too worried about it.

4

Caring

How do you care for a person who lives with the complex grief of losing someone to suicide? Much has been written to help caregivers and potential caregivers know how to come alongside those in grief (and know what to avoid!). I won't presume to fill any gaps in that literature. When I read or hear advice on what to do, I see lots of attention given to what NOT to do, such as hurtful, thoughtless comments and glib uses of Scripture. It's more challenging to know what we CAN do and should do. The tempting and tragic default is passivity motivated by fear of doing or saying something hurtful. Awkwardness and uncertainty can paralyze us, resulting in the painful isolation of those who need care the most.

Approaching the early days and weeks after Bob's death, I wondered how those around me, co-workers and friends, would respond. I had no doubt that they would hurt and care for me deeply, but I wondered how they would express it. For years I've heard an endless string of accounts from other sufferers about how well-meaning people actually reopened wounds or dug them deeper by their thoughtless remarks. I was grateful, pleased, and a bit surprised, to experience none of that.

If others felt uncomfortable around me, I was generally unaware of it. Nobody attempted to trivialize or dilute my loss by throwing Bible verses at it. Nobody referred to some greater purpose of God's, as if to make the tragedy merely a link in some grand design God is unfolding. Overall, nobody pasted an inappropriate smiley face on the situation. Yes, I understand that Scripture has the defining voice for our loss. I know that there are theological arguments for how God's sovereignty relates to our loss. Sympathy cards, emails, and text messages are simply not the place for those observations. I'm grateful that so many people in my life knew better.

Some may feel that I can't relate to their experience because I have been cared for well in my grief. I was not subjected to either glib, awkward comments or the inattention that so many others have endured. With respect and deference to all who have been treated insensitively, I think it needs to be acknowledged that sometimes people do behave with remarkable wisdom, sensitivity, and grace. May their tribe increase! I don't know what more people should have said or done that they did not. The care my family and I received was not perfect. But I have no complaints.

I have little that is new or profound to say about how to care for those who must live with the deep and complex loss involved in a suicide. Care should be thoughtful, but need not be complicated. We simply need others periodically to ask how it's going, then be willing either to listen for a while or give us the freedom not to talk about it if we're not in the mood. An occasional, random note expressing love and prayerful concern means a lot. Don't say you know how it feels, even if you think you do. If you've been through something similar, it's fine to mention that, but respect the sacredness of every person's loss by not assuming too much familiarity with what they feel. Simply saying "I'm so sorry" means a lot more. Finally, don't feel awkward about bringing up the subject. Often those of us on this side of the loss want a chance to talk about it. If you're unsure whether we want to talk, offer us the freedom not to talk about it. That type of sensitivity creates a safe and hospitable space for us, whatever our mood.

Remember that those of us left behind may experience intense mixed feelings such as wanting others to know what happened, yet hesitating to communicate the details to just anyone. Some of us will only communicate that our loved one died, yet be quite selective with whom they tell that it was a suicide. We may hesitate from a sense of shame or embarrassment. We may have emotions that are still so painful that it's simply too frightening or draining to revisit the details, especially in random conversations. Or, we may simply not have the energy to get into the subject again, at times because we're feeling good and don't want to head down that trail emotionally. The mix of emotions that we feel is complex and confusing—even for us. We do not feel the same way all the time and we may send mixed signals about what we want or need.

The experience of a loving community can also be a mixed blessing. Don't be surprised if we withdraw or seem removed now and then—or for a stretch of time—even from those who know the story and care the most. Most likely it's because we don't have the energy to respond to questions about how we're doing. Please don't be offended. It doesn't necessarily indicate that anyone has done something offensive or inappropriate. It doesn't necessarily mean that we're really fragile. We simply don't want to revisit the topic at the time. If that sounds weird, just remember that weird is what we're dealing with on a regular basis.

I hope this will not make you feel even less confident of what to do or say. It's awkward for everyone. And that does not mean that anyone is doing something wrong. It means that none of us was made for this. God made us for better. So, don't worry. Keep loving us and praying for us and inviting us and acting normal around us. Even if we sometimes seem not to be ourselves (we're not), we'll be alright. The healing has its own pace for everyone. While it cannot be hurried, it does move along.

Caring well involves a second concern with a slightly different focus—the potential suicide victims themselves; those who are somewhere on the trajectory that could lead to despair and self-destruction. Since Bob's death I have thought often about those in our world, specifically those in my circle of contacts, who may at this moment be making decisions that will someday backfire on them; or those whose psychological state is spiraling downward at a slow rate; or those who for countless other reasons are slowly headed toward a place where they feel trapped and hopeless, sensing no escape.

The struggles of these individuals are sometimes unknown even to those who know them best. They have learned how to hide their pain or they never have learned how to share it. They think they can handle their turmoil or mistakes by themselves or they are too ashamed to make it known and assume they can keep it safely contained within themselves. I'm sure there are numerous other reasons that the struggles of those who are slowly dying inside remain hidden from those who could care for them in ways that would make a difference. That makes preventative care immensely difficult and complex. But prevention is my concern.

Well-trained psychologists and counselors have provided helpful guidance on how to spot the warning signs that a person is suicidal. Certainly, we should pay attention to these. However, not every person who is on a suicidal path emits those signals. For some, the path is slow and subtle, especially difficult to detect when they are adept at masking their struggles. This does not downplay the importance of identifying and addressing the early warning signs of a potential suicidal. By all means, that must be done and done well. That is simply not the whole picture of meaningful preventative care.

I have in mind the type of preventative care that people need long before they are at risk of making a fatal decision, long before any indicators are manifest. This is tricky because we can never know exactly who might be in need of such preventative care. Unlike some forms of care, suicide prevention does not always depend on identifying the person at risk. That's actually good news in a sense. This type of preventative care can hit a broad range of people so that they never get to the danger point.

Philip Yancey once recounted a time when he asked his pastoral counselor whether he ever got tired of people like himself complaining about their petty struggles. The pastor answered by musing, "I sometimes wonder what might have happened if a skilled, sensitive person had befriended the young, impressionable Adolf Hitler as he wandered the streets of Vienna in his confused state. The world might have been spared all that bloodshed—spared

Dachau."[1] Numerous times I have told that story to my students to make the point that much of the impact of their pastoral ministries will be preventative in nature. There are no metrics for that type of transformative work. That is, they will have no way of knowing what evil is NOT committed, what harmful words are NOT spoken, what stupid decisions are NOT made as a result of what they invest in people. The cause-effect connections are untraceable in this life. I remain convinced, however, that these hidden lines of impact are among our most powerful acts of love and service. Not much new here except a heightened realization of how astonishingly significant are the simple acts of *seeing, hearing,* and *taking seriously* every person.

In his novel *Godric,* Frederick Buechner offers poignant imagery for the power of being seen. When Godric is an old man he still grieves his father, Aedlward, who had died many years prior. He grieves in part because he can't remember his father's face, but only his back. Godric's defining memories of his father are of his father walking away to work.[2] He grieved because he wanted to be seen by this highly significant person in his life. Few things are more debilitating to us as persons than feeling invisible. To feel invisible is to feel oneself to have no significance or value. Lacking the sense that one's life is significant reinforces the sense that one's death would not be all that significant either. Those feelings may be irrational and unfounded, but the effects are devastating.

I offer two suggestions as we interact with all kinds of people, some of whom may be slowly moving down a path that could eventually include serious consideration of suicide. First, we must trust that God uses little, seemingly innocuous acts to make a substantial impact on others. We need not be aware of the influence or be able to trace it. It still happens. We know this because so many of us can look back on our own lives and see the difference made by little acts of kindness or recognition that reinforced our worth, gave us hope, turned us one-tenth of a degree in a direction that averted disaster or allowed us to flourish.

1. Yancey, "Dachau—and a Pastoral Call," 80.

2. Buechner, *Godric*, 9-10.

Only in eternity might God let us see the effects of our efforts. It's making a point to ask one more question than politeness demands; to listen a little longer; to take a bit more initiative; to offer a word of genuine encouragement; to write a note of gratitude; to model a godly decision; to take a person seriously even when their struggles seem petty; to give hope through one's presence. Countless other acts could be listed, all compiling to diffuse a little bit of despair, illuminate life-preserving options, fuel a bit of hope, and give reassurance that God can be trusted.

I will probably never know in this life what *would* have prevented my brother from taking his own life, either at that fateful moment or way back upstream. Yet, I'm confident about the kind of acts that *can* have that literally life-giving effect as God mercifully uses them in that manner. Even if I don't know what's going on in the deepest chambers of another person's life, I want to give as many of those gifts as possible. I know how life-giving and valuable they are to me when others give them!

Caring well takes place all up and down the spectrum of life's struggles, from the seemingly benign to the acutely risky. Of course, when we suspect a person is struggling or on the cusp of danger we must find the courage to ask the hard questions; to intervene. In doing so we may experience avoidance, rejection, or deception. We may miscalculate or misinterpret. Yet, the hard question about how a person is really, truly doing may also open the door just enough for that person to let some help and hope enter. In these cases or those less tenuous, each of us bears the sacred duty and privilege of communicating the grace by which God preserves, directs, and saves lives. That powerful, lifesaving work can occur every day, in all kinds of ways, with all kinds of people.

Caring well is not a sophisticated craft reserved for the highly trained (though training is important and I suppose this chapter is a form of training). It starts with genuinely caring; caring enough to take the "little" steps that either don't really seem that significant or take effort we don't want to invest. It involves giving thought to what it might be like to walk in that person's shoes, even if we really don't know. It means being human and humane. It means consciously asking God to guide and shape our efforts, then trusting that in fact he does put his hands on our hands, so to speak, and make something redemptive of our clumsy efforts. That, it seems to me, is caring well in the spirit of Galatians 6:2—"Bear one another's burdens, and so fulfill the law of Christ."

Conclusion

ON THIS SIDE OF Eden we still shudder from the effects of that defining moment of mistrust and defiance against God. To some extent we have all encountered those ripples in our personal lives and observed them in the broader world at various distances from our own experience. The Bible gives us language for all that so we can recognize the multi-layered, multi-dimensional implications of that moment, that "Fall." Yet, accepting that language and trusting what Scripture says about the far-reaching, complex effects of sin in our world does not immunize our senses. As those cascading and mysterious iterations of brokenness come closer and closer, we can be repeatedly stunned—almost into shock and disbelief.

Suicide presents one of the most intensified examples of the brokenness that resulted from the Fall. Regardless of circumstances and explanations that might account for it, there remains an utter irrationality, an inscrutability to the fact that life could come to this for a person whose life undoubtedly involved so much more than what led to that tragic point. That act condenses more than we can process or absorb. The questions never really stop, even if their force abates somewhat over time.

When a person takes their own life, those of us who knew and loved them find our senses assaulted in unimaginable ways. We discover new forms of pain and disorientation. The shock wave extends into places we would have thought immune or impenetrable, and into places we did not even know existed. Emotions conflict, collide, and defy simple interpretation, much less resolution. Despair can sweep across in tidal waves or pop up with fleeting randomness.

All this points out unique and vital features of the healing and redemption offered us by God for this or any other type of loss and suffering. Healing and redemption do not result in or result from answers to the countless questions that haunt us. Nor do they imply that we become immune to further pain or tears. Interestingly, healing and redemption come our way incrementally and, in the process, we are not necessarily able to define with precision what it means. I have had to think hard about those subjects even to put inadequate words to what has come my way.

God crosses our path and "shows up" with us in genuine ways. He places his name on our wounds. He puts our questions in perspective without always answering them. He highlights the goodness of life in tragic contrast to the backdrop of our losses. He offers the grace to trust, hope, and love.

Suffering always brings with it the opportunity to focus our lives. Some allow it to diffuse or distort the focus of their lives. Yet, God presents us with the opportunity (and the challenge) for our senses to become more finely calibrated and detect beauty in the most subtle places. Perhaps we ignored or missed such beauty before because our senses had not yet been tuned by the pressure of pain. Along with new fears and struggles, new delights are also possible. Those delights texture and define our loss without erasing or counterbalancing it.

With clarified focus we become more attentive to those around us, whether or not they are suffering. And we become sensitized to the reality that others are somewhere on the path that our loved one chose. We may never know who they are or where they are on that path. But knowing that the path is still being traveled, we can seek to touch anyone who crosses our own path with humanness. What they need is the humanness that by God's grace may be instrumental in rerouting them. The redirection may only be slight, but still deeply significant.

My journey with the aftermath of a suicide will never entirely end. Even after Christ fully reconciles and heals all things, this will still have happened. I don't know for sure, but it may well be that even after God has restored and recreated all things, this loss still won't disappear from my memory banks. Somehow, though, the pain will be GONE. Perhaps it will remain forever in my memory as a marker of God's redemption and as a prompter of worshipful gratitude.

Until then the road I travel will continue to take unexpected turns, moving into odd and painful places. Until then I will continue to revisit memories and be surprised at how those memories affect me. Until Christ takes away all the pain and covers all the ugliness I will cry when I need to, laugh freely, and look for those who need a bit of life breathed into them. I will deeply and gratefully enjoy the fleeting gift of this life. I will seek wisdom from God to chart the type of life that ends gracefully and nobly.

I have no way of knowing what losses lay ahead. Admittedly, I fear those losses and admit that this particular loss has inflamed that fear. Whatever lessons I have learned, growth I have experienced, or strength I have gained through my brother's suicide; these do not insulate me against fear. I wish that were the case. For all of us, those thoughts and fears must find their place in the *until*.

Until then we seek to live—and die—in a way that leaves those behind us with nothing but the best type of sadness. If you are on this path with me, whether ahead or behind me, I pray that we can join our hearts in that same venture to defy the darkness that put us on this path in the first place.

Bibliography

Buechner, Frederick. *Godric*. New York: HarperCollins, 1980.
Vanauken, Sheldon. *A Severe Mercy*. New York: HarperCollins, 1977.
Yancey, Philip. "Dachau—and a Pastoral Call." *Christianity Today* 33 (January 13, 1989) 80.

www.ingramcontent.com/pod-product-compliance
Lightning Source LLC
LaVergne TN
LVHW021621080426
835510LV00019B/2704